Wao

by

PAUL BLOUNT

THE CLUNY PRESS
ST. ASAPH
2004

First published in 2004 by

The Cluny Press
Eirianfa
The Roe
St. Asaph
Denbighshire LL17 0LU
Wales

British Library Cataloguing in Publication Data

A catalogue record for this book is available from the British Library

ISBN 0–9547610–0–6

Typeset by Discript Limited, London WC2N 4BN
Printed in England by T.J. International Limited, Padstow, Cornwall

Contents

Wao

It is that time when seasons change
when the warm summer blue skies that you wrapped me in,
and swallows sapper green give way
and autumn and winter are left before
the summer warmth, to be replaced by the winter warmth
I will receive from you
the blue skies by the blankets, woollen, wide,
swaddling and patched with
quilted puzzles and puzzled eyes so brown and deep
as the Endrich in swell, swelly, frothing rage
champagne in summer, malt in winter is
rung by bells centuries ago; in church
pre-reformed by bigotry and tree-felled
by axemen who philosophised in aphorisms.
Scorpions scribed the sea-bed dark
with no eyes to see
but we left Bath pseudo-academics
long ago; the pretence of scientific thought
and we did not think long and hard
but now my winter sun to come is lit again by you
my wonderful bear, my warmth,
through your ringed summer and winter sun
and unlike the frickle seasons nature born
my love for you will not change.

Summer Water Meadow

The long slow note of late summer morning sun,
beguiling variations in plain chant sung at nectar.
The singers variegate with loose purpose
tightening the intensity.
Sallows in the water meadow fan the warm
which traces pollen on your hair
remembered fair in the old light, cracking
time with colours powdered down.
How cold time feels made up in an idea:
an ideal picture moving across your hair
his alabaster time traced in monochrome.
Plain song holds the still
when I imagine the spindrift from your hair
and catch you in a swarm of love.

Is It Because

Is it because I suppose your beauty will not be
transposed on that trade wind which blows
across seas and ideas, across invasions of
thought when invasion occurred and I was
wrong in difficulty, and in difficulty thought
and it went wrong?

Field Of Flowers

Before the beginning, before the break
bond Viking rib split in two, you and me
you the cannel coal whale, own tone and light
alone in a chocolate minke sea
lost in sea smoke, a sealed votary
and me cast Autumn leaves inhumed to stone
to be thread like beads in a rosary
and worn with flakes of pine upon your breast
as a mark of your serendipity,
your rubbing stone twined in your memory
worn as a charm, a counterpoint to hone
the music locked inside the stone and join
your bone to my bone in a silver cross
on the threshold to our field of flowers.

Orang-Utan

I know how strong is the sea tide night
against me, incoming from the moon in your
eyes. I know it now and knew it then.
When we were washed first with that neep
spring tide, alight with beach party glow and
fired with our delight.
I know how strong is the sea tide day
against me, outgoing from the sun in your
eyes. I know. I know it now and knew it then
when we re-met and I showered your hair
with kisses and your eyes were young again
and your agile arms and mind were one
coiled around me and mine and yours.
Orang-utan arms, as in Borneo, feeded at the
fig tree.

Waves

Eyes is a movement is in waves
and it does become as a
fine dew on a morning
sun on frost on you
as you become and
became my life again

That wave in your hair
closed in my pain
and spherical that wave
a solid shape in geometry
wavy, wavy, goodbye
and what does a zebra
feel in a zoo?

Chess

I was playing through a game:
Alekhine versus Capablanca Nineteen Twenty Seven
I played their game because there was no bravado
Between the two
between the two of us
and Alekhine played a beautiful move
and I thought of you.

Stranger

It was strange standing in that square room
in a corner, a tight corner with you
a stranger
it was strange when you never spoke
and I did all the speaking
I spoke the usual mantra
meaningless
it was strange because I did not recognise
looking into your eyes
who you were
you were a stranger in a strange land
and I was lost
and meeting a stranger for the first time
could not find the words to say
how much I loved you
because you could not understand.

When Caesar Came

When Caesar came with his crew
of mercenaries, Croats and a Jew
when Caledonia he found and thought
of raid and a grand design
he met me
and you
and a ring fort built of platinum
a band of silver shimmering dew
a pond reflecting the brightest star

and Caesar knowing, moved on
and left the band of
mercury dissolving the dew and the
tear in my eye,
for you.

Glissando

When the rotary blades cut the unkindest cut
the rosary from the faith
from the rosary floral display
flamed golden shreds, a glissandi shredding
machine macho like, like me
the gold like you, yo-yo girl, up and down
me big man in and out
what a pair between Cluny and
the deep blue sea
you and me.

Indolence

Your beauty would have been described by Marvell
metaphysically, in words of
wonder written on a night starred sky.
I breath it, non descriptively. Each breath in
in-takes your scented pillow down
each breath out deposits serenity, caught
catched on indolence.
The brown river eyes. Brown trout
rainbow wooded eyes, teaked with
circles ageing the years
river washed love rolling log-rafts to
the open sea; away from me, rolling
endlessly. Logs rolling away, away from me
I marvel at your beauty; your starred serenity.

From The Sunrise And Song Bird Sing

From the sunrise and song bird sing
      the new day born for me on your love
      a chorus of love song felt against your hair,
      sun shaded,
      against your breath, the warm and before warm
      kiss of knowledge: of you.

Of space, shaped architecturally, fitting grooved channels
made older and worn by togetherness,
like the sea rubbing against the land
to the give of sunset across the earth
where I offer my love without horizon drawn
with no recognition of day length, time composed,
where suns rise and sun sets, my love is perpetual.
No old day to forget the song.

Buttressed Walls

I remember the resonance of the young male voices
against the decorative architecture, the buttressed walls
of long time ago built sturdy and cock sure.
Sure as hell, when choirs sang the joy of the death dance
and we smiled and you cried on meeting again.
Entwined in searching strands of sand and the hour
glass slept its sleep aloud with music and structural
certainty that was right and deep and true.

True knowledge as a kiss against a young girl's lips
becomes reason and the heart beats and beats and
ever so quickly beats its rhythmic chant and a
well of love overflows.

I am with you until the end of our time
and with rebirth and rebirth.

Bach Partitas

When, as I do every day, sit at
my desk and think of you
and look at the sky and pain,
I know I should not say I love you.
Bach partitas fill my mind with you
you and pain.
I want to kiss that pain away, to
end the journey from where we came.

But now all I feel is true love for you.
The partitas do not bring pain and when
Rosalyn plays I hear only beauty for
the first time in thirty years.
Expiation is running in my tears
come my love and let us be free.

But no,
we must not go to that place that first
Adam knew, when Eve was his queen
and crowned she did deceive him with her
cruel beauty.
We will walk a different road strewn
with roses and the dew of my
tears.

There Was Nae Silver

There was nae silver when we were young
running with the horses on the plain.
You were beauty, fair flowing, fast and
seal skin. I was grey. Non-descript,
navy blue. A blue cervix in male form.
A jester; a joke; a poker player.
Playing with our lives.
There was gold in your eyes when you looked at me
and now I see after thirty years that gold again.
Your eyes are gold and silver and platinum to me.
Priceless reflections mirrowed in Bach's word-games,
musically taught. Stringed tight.
I bow to you, my love.
I do not have to forgive because
Thirty years on we are one again.

T'ai chi

Howling with wolves does not matter a lot
on a full moon night when destiny
arrives at last. A long full stop
to begin a new sentence in life
lasts a long time; to read and
write and walk straight and tie
up shoelaces straight, it's a
difficult call being born in
Beijing and applauding Chairman
Mao.

The Biggest Balloon

She came because she loved him
she couldn't stay away
she couldn't say no to him,
his requests

She came in love and came to
see the wonder of it all
In the birth she thought of him
his child
theirs

She turned his head at death and
on his ear saw a tiny mark
unrecognised before
she held him close
as close as she dared
and with a hug big as the biggest
balloon you ever saw
kissed him once, twice and
twice again
he hadn't known about her lump
in the breast, which grew and
grew
and when, he at last
saw her again
he said: 'I love you
my darling bud of May.'

Above The Pit

My thoughts are private
you cannot enter that reserved place
which is a garden where water is fed
from a spring, unknown, undiscovered by man
where all things are bright and beautiful.

In the photograph I see two naked men
holding, cupping their private parts
It is spring time, behind is blossom on
the trees, their dignity
above the pit in which the bodies piled
as high as a sky scraper
and then the shot, two shots.

We Are All One And Open

We are all one and open
the open sea and sky and flow from one to another
the sea into the sky, the sky into the sea
me into you, you into me
my love is a piece of the sky, a piece of the sea,
air and water and you the fire
a brush of your scent across the night star
glittering
and the black ghost, history calls a universal song
bird, twitters its tune
long time coming,
a long love is a life of time filling the universe
space occupied by my love for you,
my darling Rainbow Wood.

Inside The Indian Shawl

My love for you is multi dimensional
and Inca absolute, indelible
inside the Indian shawl, in the dark
eyes and inside the dark more eyes,
where pain is locked and secured;
under the low Norman ceiling uplift
was thought impossible
until Gothic voices in icicle glass slits
stained a Lancelot threaded to his romantic love
under her cloth of gold,
writing madrigals on Japanese spring paper.
No Lancelot breaking Old Testament concealment,
but on that night, with quiet breaths
he kissed her hair and turned the pain
inside the shawl, and looked with love,
no romance can describe, into her eyes
once more.

Vikings

I was in a boat load of these
bastards, can you imagine
axes and the rest, T-shirts
and long haired prima-donnas
to the point of I ain't
going to pull the oars
to acres of oak in full leaf
in full lime green, it changes
later on and the wise men
long ago called the change
seasons, but the rivers
still run to the sea.

How Like Is Sin And Love

How like is sin and love
when joined with think and feel
with you and me
my sin in being what you want in me,
or what I think you want in vain
my vanity the same
my feel the transfusion spirit strong, you in me
long love sounded echoes of that other world
where masks slip, illusions fail, and measures
have no respect; the eternal spring where
my sin is encoded skin deep
by your love and forgiveness:
think is sin, feel love
had we both seen must now be blind.

Midsummer

Now, in my mid-life
at Midsummer
the night is gentle
and I, wishing to be a gentle man,
wish the night to kiss
my love for you.

Kaiteur Fall

When the news is broke
and it is confirmed
Yes, it was you in that car, train, plane
and I was told I would never see you again
do not feel saddened, my love
for I will not grieve conventionally
but will stand above the great Kaiteur Fall
will open my arms as I did on seeing you
and when as a boy in the swimming pool
did dive
but this time I will join with the swallows
of the Fall as they dive
and enjoy the spray, the sunlight
and will remember your eyes
and will be forever with you again.

Grandma

Grandma how did you know the ley lines laid
there.
Is that why Grandad was a plate layer for
fifty years, for your life. London Midland and the clock
they gave him in recognition. On the brass
bit it said: 'Forty-five years.'
I met a man on a train journey. Nice man
he said the same happened to him. Five
years short on his clock. Time ticks
by.
Back to the ley lines Grandma, which
name shall I call a goddess?

Jock

When that man,
let's call him Philip of Normandy,
cupped that piece of glass in his hand
the very last and placed it vision free
to complete his task in York's window large
on a world so soon to end.
Henry sent his mob of marbled merry men
to reform and wreck and destroy that
bond between Man and God
and so they rode north with speed and
mud and much mess to destroy
and Jock lay dying in his bed.

Bach

I am walking into paradise with my love on
my arm and Horowitz is in Carnegie Hall,
– the 1966 concerts, when we met, he was there,
and for us he is playing the Bach/Busoni
Toccata and Fugue in C major – the third movement
marked 'Fuga'. Even time. No flash and the house
comes down Beautiful Bach splashing with time
and discipline and genius.
And I kiss your hair in the lily pond at night
when stars shine bright and Blake rules the earth,
all right. And right is time and goodness is
god and we worship no pain or gain acceptance
at his feet of clay, when young was right
and our place was in time and space. No more
say 'No' again. Please.
When Bach climbed his Fuga in C major, his
majesty and glory and divinity were revealed.
A revelation I had on my arm and besotted
with love I am.

But it is on the Fuga descent Bach shows his
hand, a helping hand, with beautiful resonance on
his mind. Mind games as he codes his love on
your arm, hand and breast and I am inside
your genes, re-engineering events past, long ago,
with future speculation and gaze at your beauty
and cannot believe when a kiss was richer than a
legacy of deceit that was bad and mad and I believed
it was from you; that hurt that had to be expiated.
Drained and drowned in that tear that broke Samuel
Palmer's moon at night.
The lily pad where I lie, Ophelia-like, gazing at
your star at night and listening to Bach.

Still Life

The burr oak bowl rim full with cherries
decorated inappropriately
a spotted red cow sugared on spring grass
freshly painted with fat sherbet brush strokes
smudged by your fingers, still-born
the seed bed raked inside the cocoon.
You played with the building blocks from childhood,
drowned dresses in a Venetian lagoon
tied the threads into a single knot
and pulled the wish pelvic bone
with my head on your breast listening
to the silence between heart beats intone:
the silent gap we pass through together
snuggling among the blueberries.

Turner And Venice

Thinking of Turner and Venice
and you all mulberry and gunmetal grey.
In March, moist with mist and cloud
Mutating at different times of day
as when I blush in a bluish shade.
The city, water colour fresh and sky
that hides a perfect conceit
small grey paper sheets and sky.

Lake of Montieth

Vikings carrying boats, swimming with swans
Lake of Montieth; jays running wild.
Is it the bell-ringers as they practice after Evensong that
drains the air along which witches' sperm is carried to you?
Male witch defying; you were adroit in your acceptance speech
witchi and a language said.
In the walk of the boy was the man; his grandfather
and time before; grandma's semi-colons and
letters,
the feather flowers flow to the floor,
the audience is seductive, fishhead, stench, bleaching
your fine headed hair
crotched in numbers.
Are you my love? My last Viking?

The New Day Is As Wondrous As Before

The new day is as wondrous as before.
When the old day, yesterday, died and went
and you said goodbye it felt temporarily
like death, a quick visitor's greeting card left
suddenly, a business card.
But being big and strong and roughty tufty
I thought aloud
so the blackbird in the tree could sing the same song.
I thought aloud there is always a tomorrow
there is always a second spring where we
will go and wash away impurities and cleanse
and become one again.

Cinnamon In The Still Christian Air

There was no cinnamon in the still Christian air,
on full moon day
and you perched, rugged, weaved hair pulled around plaits,
sprung fine as a lass
my lass
my remembrance. Radiant
my kiss on the moon
there were cloves, scented blues and greens
running indiscriminately, Liszt beats
as birdwing butterflies and cages empty
emptied cinnamon in the still Christian
night air and moths falling free.
New Testament thinking
Matthew, Mark, Luke, John
Luke
there were almonds in the blues and green in your eyes.

Dante's Garden

Naming a game played by me and you
in our dream time slumber, bumble bee
strident sting awakes the memory,
shakes out the runes, ring the canto bell
in Rainbow Wood where we read the tree alphabet
and aspired to wear in the whin
a winding chain of heather gold
with your eyes and secrecy.
And I was private with the mystic second sight
as rainbows reflected your silver seal skin
tight with right, and covered you with hazelnut shells
and rubbed you with earth and moss
and licked and licked your light rayed hair
and left you there in Dante's eternal garden.

Autumn Rays Lit Rainbow Wood

I dare say
when first autumn rays lit Rainbow Wood,
before Rome and Bath,
and the she-wolf scented and stalking her bank of seed;
when she was young in her cycle of displacement
and sought provenance from Viking
king stock and Norman blood
a fool ran to the seed-sound of the horn,
ran in the rainbow to his love
by the beat of the tom-tom man.
He and the she-wolf danced an arabesque
all bit and transcendant
and on a rock she called: 'I own everything you can see.'
But he, the fool, only was listening to
Shostakovich preludes and fugues
fighting free kittens.

After Yeats's Mermaid

'How long can you hold your breath?' you once asked me.
'I'll show you,' I said, counting one, two, three.
And before you could blink or twinkle an eye
I had descended to the bottom of the sea,
and with my mouth open
wide
did prise the pearl from the sandy shady
sea
and float with that pearl for you to see.
And you did take it from my mouth
with your mouth
and the kiss of life did apply to me.
Alas too long had I dived
and a tear did fall on me.

Spring Silver Bull

Your beauty once turned did caress
my breast and as I turned did feel
a little of the distress, when you said: 'No',
but now like a young spring silver bull do know
that love is indeed in a word we both know.

Roly Poly

You are all the words there have ever been
rolled into one person
so beautiful like freedom
and freedom of thought
me thinking about you
alone, contemplatively.
Roly poly pudding and pie.

Michelangelo's Fingers

Standing on the beach where you
made quite a splash those many years ago
beach equals yellow; splash equals red
yellow girls run naked playing in the
sand drifting to sea, delicately.
Red men splash yellow girls.
Throw flat stones, across the still.

Yellow sea becomes blue;
each bounce becomes a different colour,
difficult
I once went out in snow looking
for you;
whiteout
come-back
please
it's tropical here, where verdant and
sand meet
where Michelangelo's fingers
were painted.
Colour me.

Shostakovich And Prokofiev

Champagne and snowdrops,
arthritic stems
anxiously appearing early, like new birth
before its time;
black beaver washing in the Volga
under sunlight, soft rays
after the cabaret, new morning
new revolution
a new red colour on the palette
as the beaver is cut in two.

Shostakovich and Prokofiev:
we grew as twins
we know this from the grave
too horrible to bother to change
the fresh dew idea of what it
was that coloured the bee.

Not Yet Made Man

I remember, it was a little rouge, blush pink, on your cheek
and welled brown eyes that
glowed first for me those years ago:
when, as a boy, not yet made-man, I first thirsted for you,
mind, body and soul, a hungry soul.
Pinkish: my beautiful mucky pup
rolled herring round and perfect, striped fisher wife
wifey, wifey: daft; broomstick
witchy, wifey, pinky draft, daft.
A beautiful mermaid you become
and not for me; then until the
grave, we shall share the bed rock
for eternity, for Milton; blind.

Mucky Pup

You are my first lady
my most favourite of all
knees, red cord dress
you are the day the earth was born.
My entrance to humility and warmth in your voice
the moon seemed tender and cool, the evening
all pinky and lovely and mucky pup clean
that Hallowe'en, the first with you
when the moon grew and petrified in a
'Hungarian Rhapsody' prepared by Liszt
bewitched by profundity and a man,
you left me those years ago
but I know I had left you in my disgrace of unthinking.
The screaming girls are at their ballet now
and Gilels plays the Debussy piano solo
and there are reports of good orang-utans.

Rainbow Wood

In Rainbow Wood I found my love
ran wild and together stood
where the rainbow showered
glints of laughter in her hair
and happiness between us shared
watched the autumn rainbow flame
catch us cold, level and make humane
ran wild my love and I into that rainbow,
into the rings of the wood.

Bucharest

The stars above Marrakech were
especially luminous that night
bathed as they were in their
shrinki bits and things
and as I gazed I remembered
that lone star grazed kneed
I once saw more luminous than
the rest.
I tried to remember where I gazed
at that lone star lost,
so lost and alone in our milky way
in our lost galaxy.
Now I remember: it was above
Bucharest.

Weighing Souls In Stained Glass

It was like weighing
souls in stained glass
when my love for you
fell between a last
remembrance of summers
and a fall reminiscent
of heavens descent when
Eve, taking all
left
and a stone turned to salt.

Monet

The rowans here are gathering their red resonance dots
just like we,
picked for plucking by the birds of the tree.
But, for me, bye-bye Monet
bye-bye Giverny.
I never knew that you did know, with
the electric light shining in your
wife's dead face, that you could paint at Vétheuil.

There is a point in poetry Monet,
in pointed remarks in paint.

Mon et mon lily of the valley; my mother's favourite, Monet.
Muguet; my and my lily pond; soft; fleshly reflections.
Bye-bye Vétheuil.

And the glory in your God did jerk me straight
Upright with respect for your art
and a sense, sniffing in bushes for scent after she had gone.
The Romans drew rowan buds too.

When I Was Pagan Picked

I dare say
when I was Pagan picked, in the dark green of day
and daisies were shaken yellow down;
my daisy chain ring welded by your
light and kiss
my seed new iced in your womb on winter solstice,
mummified
as the swirl of fruit bats, equatorially flew
their nightly kill
by an Arab moon
and a sailor, sea water sick, warmed your hand
under a
Christian star.

It Was The Blush Pink Lower Sky

It was the blush pink lower sky
with blue, that reminded me of you.
Over to the south it was dirty
blue, your mucky pup colour on a
bad day.
And this had been a bad day.
So thank you for your help.
I like your pink: in the sky
tonight it was a movement
with lots of show and bottle;
you are a strong sky woman.

When The Shooting Star Did Engage With Marx

When the shooting star did engage with Marx
in University days, I did find in her
very hazel brown eyes a thing
that physicists have puzzled over,
over time, like speed, and velocity
and a thing called time.
And later, when I recalled this, when
finding her again I said: 'One
wish, to envelop you not as again
but anew.' In newness, like Catholicism
re-discovered my love.

With Orwell I Knew There Is No Escape

With Orwell I knew there is no escape
and with St. Paul no forgiveness
but I did not believe there was no
new life
it came to me one day between a
cold snap
sitting in a garden as yet fully
grown, snapdragons, sublime
looked like coiled snakes raking
over old embers.

The Chinese Cup

In Yeats's china shop, one day, I found a rare cup which
held a hand of gold, and on its finger a silver ring
shone so bright it dazzled, and your smile, bamboozled,
confused, I withdrew out of your sight.

For many years my heart ached for your smile.

But Yeats was true and beauty grew.
When I returned there was that cup which had remained,
and the gold and the silver, intact.
The cup was Chinese, as in the Burrell. Early on
when potters and painters did not masquerade, but drew
their pots and coloured them with love.

My cup was pink: the pink of everlasting dawns
when swans and the dawn rise eternally.

Kantor's Kiss

There is a grove in Arcadia
where olives long of old time
and mathematicians did thrive
and make their speculations about
things and that and rats ran
round a clock Newton called
between space and time where
Kantor stood his ground.

There is a grove in Arcadia
where Alicia born did spring that
point in infinity did create that
pool in which a reflection was born
and I saw you the first time,
the first kiss, that point in infinity
my first kiss to you,
and your child to her and you
I give Kantor's kiss
for the ever disbelief he saw.

Poppies

I am a meteor from outside space
I fly faster than fast can describe
and arrive stiller than the stillest pond can
look in dappled shade light.
I am sperm, male driving home,
to embed inside your inner being
to which Freud was a foreign land
with poppies, red and happy.

There Is A Trace In The Universe

There is a trace in the universe
like jet stream, it makes the rivers on earth
glow blue and muddy brown
it made the fingers on your hand
the wedding finger on your left hand
my ring.
Wagner.

In The Moment Of Our Most Troubled Thoughts

In the moment of our most troubled thoughts
when the sunlight, bright through
windows to the west did shine
and refine my thoughts and the Jesus child did cry
in his Moses basket so crude that Islam
was allowed to leak in

And falling as sinking angels do
sink and fall and bash
their heads
against the earth, I was left alone
and alone without you
did descend into that area of
uncertainty on rocks bereft

In the moment of our most troubled thoughts
one thought against the dragon,
strengthened me and my sword and
was swift in its despatch
that enemy had two to face: me and you

But dragon roused born and dragon coloured could not believe
in St. George, his
colours lit large the Red, the White, the Blue
because in Dragon Land there were no colours
he knew

only the colour of death and
no colour chart showed that.

Constable's Clouds

I see you in every cloud
the sky white: white clouds, the linen bed clouds
the white grey clouds, grey clouds; the white grey clouds.
I see you in every cloud, mixed with anxiety.

I see your movement in the clouds
your change in the sky
your smile from white to grey to Parisien red
I see in the dark brown, brown clouds, your eyes
I see you in every cloud
every haunting cloud shaped around your eyes
I see you.

I see Davide in your red cloud lips
frightened for you and me
and Géricault in your moon side not shown to me
and Raphael in his clouds of virginity wet with the divine child

in you I see streams of clouds dissolved in the
rich brown earth pools in your eyes
the unification of earth, sky and me to you.